Dairy Produce

From the time when mankind first turned from hunter to farmer, the dairy cow has provided the human race with one of its most valuable sources of nourishment. Once people had learned to tame the wild ancestors of the modern cow, they kept them for milk to begin with, and then learned how to make cheese and butter. Because of their role as providers, cows were often especially valued by their keepers and in many parts of Africa a man's wealth is still judged by the number of cattle he possesses. But where once the world's farmers kept a few cows to feed the family, with a little left over for sale, dairy farming and the manufacture of dairy products is now a very important, world-wide industry which supports millions of people – and helps to feed many millions more. Richard Clark has been a newspaper, magazine and television writer for 35 years, but more recently he has concentrated on writing about the production of natural commodities and crops, and the industries based on them.

Focus on
DAIRY PRODUCE

Richard Clark

Focus on Resources series

Alternative Energy
Coffee
Cotton
Dairy Produce
Gas
Grain
Nuclear Fuel
Oil
Seafood
Sugar
Tea
Timber
Water
Wool

Frontispiece   *A display of the wide range of Danish dairy produce.*

First published in 1985 by
Wayland (Publishers) Ltd
49 Lansdowne Place, Hove
East Sussex BN3 1HF, England

Phototypeset by Kalligraphics Ltd, Redhill, Surrey
Printed in Italy by G. Canale & C.S.p.A., Turin
Bound in Great Britain at The Bath Press, Avon

British Library Cataloguing in Publication Data

Clark, Richard
  Focus on dairy produce. – (Focus on resources
  series)
  1. Dairy products – Juvenile literature
  I. Title
637   SF250.5

ISBN 0–85078–601–0

Contents

1. The perfect food   6
2. Milk from many sources   8
3. The first herdsman   10
4. The great Pasteur   12
5. The industrial dairy farm   14
6. From farm to table   16
7. The daily miracle   18
8. Milk in many forms   20
9. Making cream and butter   22
10. Naughty – but nice!   24
11. Man-made substitutes   26
12. From milk to cheese   28
13. Hundreds of cheeses   30
14. Yoghurt – secret of long life?   32
15. Sweet delights   34
16. The great diet debate   36
17. Lakes and mountains   38
18. Dairy organizations   40
19. Strawberries or cream?   42

Facts and figures   44
Glossary   46
Books to read   47
Index   48

1. The perfect food

At the very beginning of their lives all mammals, including baby human beings, depend on milk for their lives. The perfect kind is, of course, provided by their own mothers because it is of exactly the right composition, pure, always the right temperature, and always handy.

There are certain substitutes which can be used if, for any reason, mother's milk is not available. These give all the correct nutritional ingredients, but medical thinking these days is that babies receive a certain amount of protection from various ailments through their own mother's milk.

It is certainly true that milk from all mammals is highly nutritious because it contains butterfat, nourishing proteins, milk sugar, almost all the minerals and natural salts the body needs regularly, and certain important vitamins. Together these provide energy and help to build strong bones and teeth as well as muscle,

All mammals, including human beings depend on their mother's milk at the start of their lives. Here is a Jersey cow and her young calf.

Most British householders have their milk delivered every morning by milkmen.

so for centuries milk has been regarded as an essential part of the diet of growing children. In recent years, though, there have been doubts raised about the possible dangers to health of a diet that is too high in fat.

For most people in the Western, industrialized nations, the main milk producer is the familiar domestic cow. Originally all cows were kept as much for the calves they could produce as for their milk; bull calves with their male glands removed were raised to pull ploughs and carts, or to be used for meat. Later, when the appetite for drinking milk, butter and cheese and pure cream grew, farmers began to rear breeds which produced large amounts of milk; other breeds of cow were developed purely for their meat.

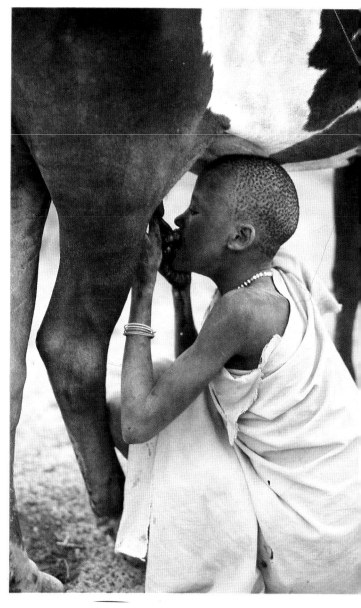

A Dinka boy, from Sudan, suckling milk from a cow's teat. Milk is very nutritious — full of minerals and vitamins.

7

2. Milk from many sources

Cows are not the only milk-providers that mankind has domesticated over the centuries. As a matter of fact, there are people in some parts of the world who actually become very ill if they drink cow's milk, because their stomachs are not used to it. In many countries this has happened because the climate and other natural conditions, including diseases and insect pests, have made it impossible to rear cows.

It would, for instance, be difficult to keep cows in hot desert conditions or in high mountain country where grass and other suitable fodder is not available. Nevertheless, goats can flourish on even the dryest bushes in the hot climates of many African countries, as well as on the tough vegetation high in the mountains of France and Switzerland. Sheep, too, produce a very rich milk on poor pasture.

Even more hardy, yaks and llamas provide milk for Tibetans high in the Himalayan mountains and South American Indians in the Andes mountains. The wandering Bedouin and other tribes in Saudi Arabia and North Africa milk their camels, as well as ride on them. In Mongolia and parts of the USSR, nomadic herdsmen, who travel on horseback, milk the mares.

In terms of sheer numbers, though, it is probably fair to say that next to cows the most common milk-producing animal is the water buffalo. This is not the ferocious beast that used to roam the North American plains in vast herds, but the type that is familiar in all parts of India, the Far East and the Pacific countries where it is also used to work in the water-logged ricefields. In Italy, too, buffalo milk, which is high in butterfat, is used to produce very special cheeses.

Left *Cows are not the only milk-providers. Here a camel is being milked in Mongolia.*

A nomadic tribesman on the Afghan-Pakistani border milking one of his goats.

3. The first herdsman

The first person ever to milk a cow must have been brave, because it was probably a very wild one, with needle-sharp horns to fight off hungry hunting animals. Nobody can be sure when it happened, but some clay models of what look reasonably like a modern cow, made many thousands of years ago, have been found. This suggests that cattle at least were tamed for mankind's use in the very remote past. The same is probably true for all the other milk-producing animals.

However it happened, it could not have been long before people learned that milk in the natural state was a short-lived product. It was fine when it was fresh but smelly and useless after a few days, especially in hot weather. It was probably kept in skin 'bottles', earthenware pots or dried and hollowed-out gourds which were seldom washed, so that the milk soon turned sour.

It is almost certain that the secret of turning milk into something more solid and long-lived was discovered by accident when someone noticed that milk kept in a skin bottle, made from a calf or a lamb's stomach, formed into curds that could be drained and shaped into a lump, instead of just going bad. The reason, as we now know, is that young animals have a substance called rennet in their stomachs to help them digest milk and an extract of rennet is still added to warm milk to produce cheese to this

Left *The first herdsmen kept their milk in hollowed-out gourds like the one from which this Dinka baby is drinking.*

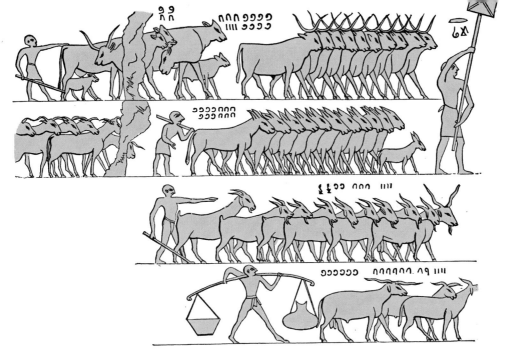

Thousands of years ago, the Egyptians made cheese from cows' milk.

day. Paintings and carvings made in Egypt and the Middle East four to five thousand years ago show farm slaves making cheese.

The discovery of butter was probably made at about the same time. People riding on horseback, who carried milk with them, found that after it had been jogged about for a certain length of time, lumps formed. Later on they realized that the magic worked even quicker if they only used the thick cream that rose to the top after the milk had been left standing for a while, and that it lasted even better if you added a little salt.

Left *A milkmaid hand-milking an ewe in the Middle Ages.*

4. The great Pasteur

A nineteenth-century advertisement for a dairy in London, which used a handcart to distribute milk.

The processes of cheese and butter making were refined over the centuries, of course, but because nothing could be done to preserve drinkable milk for more than a few days, people had to rely on nearby farms for their supplies or, in the case of town-dwellers, on local dairies. This state of affairs lasted until the late nineteenth century.

Not only did milk go 'off' too quickly, but bovine diseases including tuberculosis and brucellosis could be transmitted to humans through it. As a natural product, milk was also a host for many germs. Although strict rules of cleanliness on dairy premises, including sterilization of all churns, bottles and other equipment, eventually ensured that the product was reasonably pure, it was still not one hundred per cent safe.

In the circumstances, milk distribution on a wider scale remained something of a problem even after the new railway networks cut transport times drastically. It was the great French scientist, Louis Pasteur, who made the modern milk industry possible.

Pasteur, who lived from 1822 to 1895, had been called in by the French wine industry to find a method of preventing wine from going sour. Pasteur proved that the souring of the wine was caused by bacteria which grew in it. He then showed that heating it to a high temperature would destroy all these dangerous organisms. The process, now applied to almost all milk produced in more advanced countries, is still called 'pasteurization': milk is heated briefly to about 70°C (158°F).

This milkmaid distributed milk around her village in the early 1820s.

5. The industrial dairy farm

Right up until the beginning of this century, farming was still a small-scale business using non-industrial methods. The dairy business, in particular, was a major employer of labour because cows had to be hand-milked and, in much of the world, cheese and butter were still mainly produced with small, hand-operated implements.

Milk, butter, cheese and all the other dairy products are now almost entirely processed by mechanical methods and they are produced on such a scale, world-wide, that they must now be classed as a farm 'crop' like wheat, sugar, and fruit. Butter and cheese, especially, are major sources of income for countries like New Zealand, the Netherlands, Denmark and Ireland.

Dairy farming is preferred to beef ranching, even in countries like the USA and Argentina where gigantic herds tended by cowboys or 'gauchos' used to provide half the world with meat. Dairy farming takes up less room because cows can feed on both well-fertilized pasture grass on small farms in the summer and on grain or silage in winter and so produce milk all the

Ways of organizing the flow of cows through a milking parlour. **Below** *The cows circulate on a large turntable.* **Below right** *The most common form of milking parlour.*

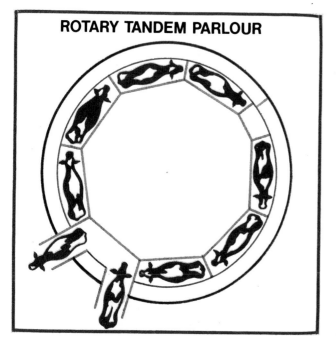

ROTARY TANDEM PARLOUR

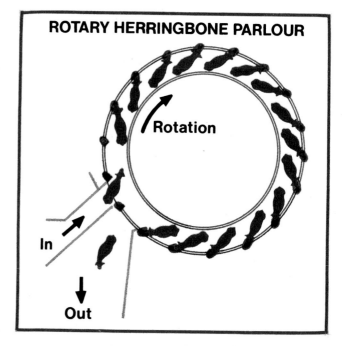

ROTARY HERRINGBONE PARLOUR

Rotation

In

Out

year round. Milking machines in the dairy and large tankers instead of old-fashioned milk churns help to cut labour costs. For every tonne of butter or cheese produced by direct human labour fifty years ago, today's gleaming stainless-steel equipment, all automatically controlled by a few white-coated engineers, will produce a thousand tonnes.

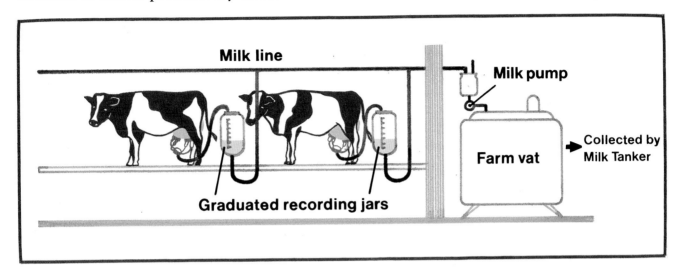

Above *The amount of milk that each cow produces is recorded.*

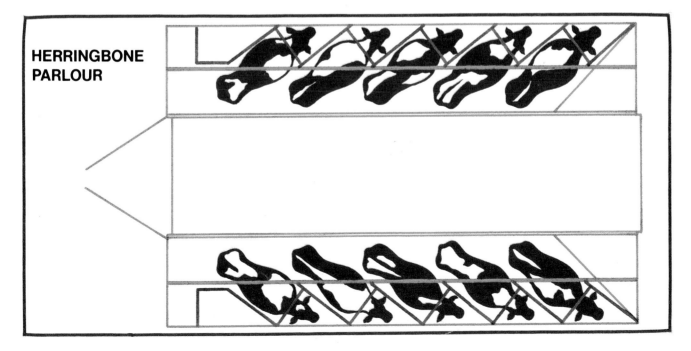

HERRINGBONE PARLOUR

6. From farm to table

In the past, dairies were always near their customers, but the growth of the world's cities made it impossible to operate even the smallest farm within their boundaries. Getting the milk from farm to customer is now a highly complicated and expensive procedure, and only modern packaging methods and fast transport make it possible.

Today the milk is often pasteurized on the farms and then collected by large milk tankers which take it to the nearest storage and bottling centre or creamery. Here it is either bottled or forwarded in even bigger road or rail tankers to the nearest town or city bottling depot. After very strict tests for quality and total cleanliness, it is usually stored in enormous stainless-steel tanks before being packed for final delivery.

In many countries, the milk bottle is still the most favoured method of transporting milk, and it is one that has some obvious advantages. The bottles are tough enough to be used several times, and the customers can see what they are buying. Also, the bottles can be steam-cleaned for total hygiene. But, increasingly, specially treated cardboard cartons are taking over from the bottle. They are cheap, and because they are only used once, the dairy companies do not have to worry about getting them back and cleaning them for re-use.

Most milk sales in the rest of the world are made from supermarket shelves, and supermarket companies lack both the staff and the organization to recycle milk bottles. In Britain and New Zealand, milk is still delivered door to door each day.

Left *In this pasteurization plant, milk is heated to 72°C (162°F) for 15 seconds and then rapidly cooled to 4°C (40°F).*

Above *A milk-bottling plant in operation in New Zealand.* **Below** *New Zealand is one of the few countries in the world where milk can still be delivered to your door.*

7. The daily miracle

All these modern developments sometimes make it easy to overlook the importance of the cow as the foundation of this massive industrial and commercial enterprise.

In fact, the cow has also evolved over the centuries and today's breeds are far more efficient producers of milk than their ancestors. What is more, different breeds of dairy cow produce different types of milk. Jerseys, Guernseys and South Devons all produce very rich milk with a high butterfat content; while Friesians produce a greater volume of milk with less butterfat in it. What they all do is to convert their food into milk very efficiently indeed.

Cows tear off the grass or eat the special winter protein feed – 70 kg (154 lbs) a day – from a trough and, swallowing quickly, store the food in the first two of their four-compartment stomachs. From time to time, they force this 'cud' back up into their mouths and chew it before swallowing the finely ground particles back into the first two compartments where the digestive juices get to work. Surplus water is later removed in the third compartment and final digestion takes place in the fourth.

The nutritious elements are removed in the cow's intestines and passed into the blood. This not only feeds the cells of the body but also produces milk when it is passed through groups of tiny cells in the milk bag, or udder. Each tiny

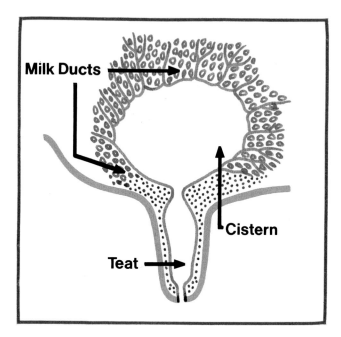

A cross-section of a cow's teat. Blood carries nutrients to the udder. Here small spongy cells, called alveoli, make the milk. The droplets of milk pass through ducts to four cisterns, above each of the teats, where they are stored.

droplet of milk eventually reaches the storage ducts which supply the four teats. Hand-milking, which involves squeezing and pulling the teats is a highly skilled and tiring procedure; the suction-operated milking machine, developed in the 1860s is cleaner and more efficient.

Above *A herd of Friesians in New Zealand.* **Below** *This diagram shows the four compartments of a cow's stomach. Food is stored in the rumen and reticulum. From the rumen, small amounts of unchewed food return to the mouth. They are then returned to the omasum, where surplus water is removed, before passing on to the abomasum. Here the food is broken down by the stomach juices.*

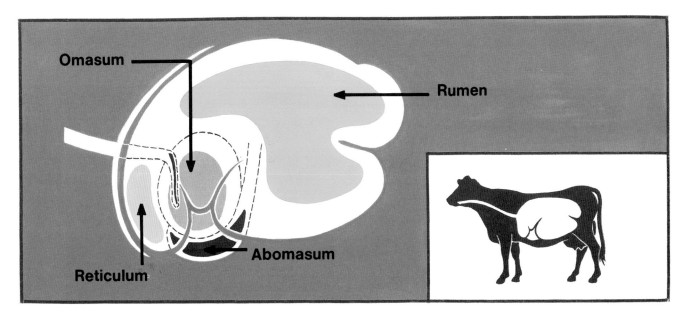

8. Milk in many forms

Varieties of milk.

In some countries, including Britain, the milk that is delivered or sold from shops is a fairly straight-forward product in which the cream content rises to the top. But in most of Europe, in the USA and in many other parts of the world, the milk is homogenized; that is, it is forced at great pressure through a tiny sprayhole so that the tiny globules of fat are broken up and distributed evenly throughout the milk. This makes it seem smoother and more creamy-tasting, as well as easier to digest.

In many countries, too, UHT (Ultra Heat Treatment) milk is favoured because the very high heat to which it is exposed – longer than for ordinary pasteurization – means that it will stay fresh in its specially sterile cardboard containers for many months without needing refrigeration. Sterilized milk, which is treated with heat after being sealed in bottles, was once fairly popular because it lasted a long time, but it tends to taste 'cooked'.

In countries where diseases, like rinderpest, make it difficult to keep dairy cattle, powdered milk has been used for many years. To make this, milk is sprayed in fine jets on to the sides of a heated steel tank where it dries out and turns to a powder.

Below *UHT milk in a Kenyan dairy.*

In most countries, milk in cartons is replacing bottled milk.

Two other types of milk are condensed milk and evaporated milk. Condensed milk is first of all homogenized, and sugar is added to it. It is then heated to a high temperature for a short time, before being pumped into a vacuum tank, where it is boiled until it thickens to about two and a half times its original consistency. Evaporated milk is made in a similar way, except that no sugar is added, and the final product is not quite so thick.

9. Making cream and butter

The simplest way of making butter is to let milk stand in a wide pan until the cream, which contains the butterfat and is lighter than the rest of the fluid, rises to the top. This top layer is then very carefully skimmed off and poured into a butter churn. This has rotating paddles that beat the cream until it sets into a lump.

In the 1800s, cream was hand 'churned' in barrels, like this one, to form butter.

A modern butter-making machine.

That, more or less, is the way it was done for centuries and in many parts of the developing world it is still churned by hand. But in a modern creamery, the milk is first heated and then fed into a high-powered separator. A factory-sized separator has a huge stainless-steel bowl inside a metal casing and the bowl is spun furiously at 6,000 revolutions a minute. Inside the bowl there is a stack of cone-shaped metal plates with tiny gaps between each. The milk comes through minute holes in the plates and the spinning plates fling the heavier skimmed milk out towards the edges of the bowl, letting the lighter cream flow down towards the centre.

The cream is stored in glass-lined or stainless-steel tanks at a fixed temperature of 4.5°C (40°F) to let the fat globules 'set'. To make butter, the cream has to be churned into a solid mass from which the thin buttermilk is allowed to drain before being replaced with chilled water to wash the butter grains. The butter is then 'worked' to produce an even texture; some butters have salt added.

This whole, complicated process is carried out without a pause in modern butter-making equipment, and it ends with the butter being fed in one long ribbon to the packaging

Below *These machines separate the cream from the skimmed milk.*

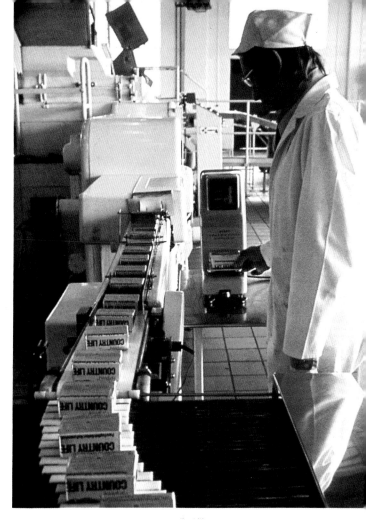

Packs of butter coming out of the wrapping machine.

machines where it is cut and wrapped in metal foil or waxed paper.

'Sweet' butter cooks better than salted butter because it tends not to burn too easily. Many Asian people like butter which has been clarified. It is melted and the solids which rise to the top are skimmed off. It is known as ghee.

23

10. Naughty – but nice!

Life would be very boring if all we were allowed to eat were foods which were good for us, or very plain. Because it is so very rich in fats, cream is sometimes thought to be a little wicked, but on the other hand it has to be admitted that it is also a very special treat in cakes or on hot buttered scones with jam, on waffles with maple syrup, in very rich sauces, added to ice-cream dishes, and floated on coffee or drinking chocolate.

The two main types of cream are called, simply, single or double and as the description suggests, single is thinner than double, with a lower fat content. This is the cream that you add to sauces to make them more tasty and which you can pour on fruit salads. Double cream is the one which you whip by hand with a wire whisk or in an electrically operated blender

Delicious Danish pastries, containing double cream, being made in a bakery in Denmark.

until it is almost solid, before using it to fill cakes or pastries like chocolate éclairs.

In recent years, two other varieties of cream have made their appearance on the supermarket shelves, and the main one is called 'whipping cream'. This is not quite as rich as double cream but, unlike single cream, it can be whipped until it is light and fluffy and it can then be used in much the same way as whipped double cream. The other, much used in cafés, is cream which is squirted from an aerosol can on to milk shakes and coffee.

A lot of sour cream is used in Europe, especially stirred into soups like the Russian bortsch or to give a special tang to sweet jam pancakes. Buttermilk, too, can be processed into a slightly sour and thick product called Smetana and this can be used in much the same way as sour cream.

Naughty but nice

Below *Varieties of cream, including single, double and whipping; in tins as well as in the more familiar cartons.*

11. Man-made substitutes

Most of the products which have been created as substitutes for real dairy products were designed to provide either cheaper or longer-lasting alternatives. Before the days of refrigeration and totally sterile methods of manufacture, butter was very much a luxury product and, apart from farmers who could make their own, only fairly well-to-do people could afford to use it regularly. To provide a nutritious spread which poorer people could buy, scientists produced margarine by treating vegetable fats with various chemicals and adding substances, which are known as emulsifiers to produce a solid product.

The original margarine was pale white, and dairy industries all over the world fought long

Many people have stopped using butter in favour of man-made substitute spreads like these.

THE COUNTRY LIFE BUTTER MEN

This advertisement was part of a publicity campaign to keep people eating butter.

legal battles to prevent the manufacturers from adding colour dyes to make it look like butter. In the USA some 30 years ago, margarine was still being sold with colouring dyes in a separate capsule, to be mixed in at home.

It has also been common for many years for the makers of cheaper cakes and pastries to use artificial cream as a filler. This can vary from the relatively rich 'custard' made by thickening plain milk with eggs or egg powder to a product based on corn or potato flour, with colour and flavouring added.

In parts of the world like Asia, where drinking milk has never been as popular as it is in the USA and Europe, people have for years been drinking a 'milk' which is made from vegetable products like soya beans. This does not pretend to be real milk, but it is enjoyed as a healthy drink in its own right. However, vegetable-based 'coffee creamers' are becoming increasingly used in Western countries because they are convenient, easy to store and low in fat. They can also be used in vending machines, which cannot store fresh milk.

12. From milk to cheese

Turning milk into cheese is, as we now know, the oldest, the most natural and certainly one of the tastiest ways of preserving the nourishing contents of milk. To make the change, the single most important item is rennet and although most cheeses are still made with a natural rennet extracted from the stomach linings of young animals, there is a vegetable rennet which vegetarians – who eat no meat or meat products – prefer.

The process begins with milk, which can be from cows, buffaloes, goats or sheep, which is heated to destroy any harmful germs or bacteria. It is then pumped into cheese vats which,

The curds and whey being separated.

The first stage in making Emmental cheese.

in the big cheese factories, can hold up to 22,500 litres (4,950 gallons). The rennet is added and it acts with the natural acid in the milk to form thick curds. After about half an hour, the curds are thick enough to cut into small pieces, which are then heated and stirred to force out the thin, watery whey.

Next, the curd is allowed to settle at the bottom of the vat and the whey is run off. In

making hard, Cheddar-type, cheeses, the curds are cut into blocks and stacked on either side of the vat to allow full draining before being cut up into chip-size pieces in a mill. The curd is salted and packed into a mould where it is pressed for about a day and then wrapped in cloth or plastic film, or covered in wax, before being left to ripen.

The ripening period varies, depending on the type of cheese, but unripened cheese usually tastes of nothing at all.

Unlike the hard cheeses, the soft curd cheeses, made from milk which has turned sour either naturally or because acids have been added, need to be eaten soon after they have been made. They are often known as cottage cheeses, and they are moist and crumbly.

Below *The final product: Emmental cheeses maturing and ripening.*

13. Hundreds of cheeses

When he was President of France, the late General de Gaulle is said to have exclaimed during a time of political trouble: 'Who can hope to run a country that produces over 400 different cheeses!' It is certainly true that France is the cheese-making champion of the world. Almost every region seems to produce its own special

cheese. Famous French cheeses include Camembert, Brie, and Roquefort, a strong blue cheese made from ewes' milk.

Britain has the sturdy Cheddar, Cheshire, Lancashire, Wensleydale, Gloucester and the famous blue Stilton, with Dunlop from Scotland and Caerphilly from Wales.

The Dutch eat cheese for breakfast. Their great specialities are the cannonball-shaped Goudas and wheel-shaped Edams. Like the Dutch, the Danes have a huge dairy industry and they produce over 50 varieties of cheese. In Italy they have been making cheese since Roman times. The most famous Italian cheese is Parmiggiano – or Parmesan.

It is impossible, too, to overlook the contribution of tiny Switzerland to the world's cheese culture. It is one of the great dairy countries, and the most familiar sound still in many parts of rural Switzerland is the tinkle of cow bells. Gruyère and Emmental are among its most famous products.

In sheer quantity, though, the world's leading cheesemakers are the USA, Canada and – in proportion to their small populations – New Zealand and Australia.

Left *Parmesan cheeses ripening. Cheese has been made in Italy since Roman times.*

Some of the wide varieties of cheeses on sale in a British supermarket.

14. Yoghurt – secret of long life?

Look at the dairy products section of any supermarket and what you will notice most are hundreds of plastic pots of yoghurt. Some are plain, most have fruit included, but all of them are sold in billions of units a day all over the world. Nowadays it seems impossible to imagine a time when this was not the case, but the truth is that yoghurt only became widely popular about 30 years ago.

Until then, yoghurt had been considered mainly as a dish for simple peasant farmers. But then stories began to circulate among health food fans that farmers in countries like Bulgaria and the USSR, who ate huge amounts of yoghurt, lived to incredible ages. Well, there was a certain amount of exaggeration, but many doctors do agree that yoghurt is a good food. Once it had been discovered that the appeal of what seemed to many people to be nothing more than thick sour milk could be improved by adding fruits and flavourings, the big dairy companies began to make it.

The simple recipe for plain yoghurt involves warming milk to blood heat and then adding a type of harmless bacteria, called *Lactobacillus bulgaricus*, and keeping the mixture warm until it sets solid. There are electric yoghurt makers for use at home, but a wide-mouthed vaccum flask like the ones you keep drinks warm in can also be used. The yoghurt bacteria actually grows when in use and ends up looking a bit like a cauliflower floret, but you can also use a small amount of natural yoghurt mixed with the warm milk to start a new batch.

Yoghurt is made in a factory by heating up milk and then allowing it to cool to about 40°C (104°F). The bacteria is then added to ferment the milk. When the acid content reaches a certain level, the yoghurt is cooled and packed. If you look inside a fresh pot of yoghurt, you may see a small amount of watery liquid on the yoghurt's surface. This is the whey produced by the acid.

Right *Yoghurt is a very versatile food which is popular in many countries around the world. Some people eat it because they believe that it will make them live longer!*

15. Sweet delights

Did the Chinese invent ice-cream, or did the ancient Romans think of it first? Whoever it was, they have earned the gratitude of most of the world's population – and not just those of the hot nations. The Russians, for instance, make superb ice-cream and they eat it even during the worst of their winter weather. Nobody can claim that ice-cream is an essential part of a proper diet; it is a luxury, pure and simple, and one that few people can resist.

Unfortunately, most of the ice-cream that we buy today has little to do with milk, and is mainly made from fats extracted from vegetable matter. Real dairy ice-cream, buttery-yellow in

Milk chocolate sweets and Easter eggs being made in a factory in Britain.

Children queuing up to buy ice-cream in a park in New York.

colour, is very hard to find. This 'true' ice-cream is made from cream, egg yolks and sweeteners, with a flavouring like vanilla added. This is stirred continually while it is freezing so that there are no big ice crystals in the finished product, which should be rich and smooth.

Factory-made ice-cream consists of powdered milk, sugar and other additives mixed with liquid milk, sugar and fats. This mixture is pasteurized and homogenized, and then left to 'age' for four hours to settle. It is then frozen, moulded and packed in a variety of ways — for cones, family packs or for bulk selling.

The other popular sweet favourite is dairy milk chocolate, which was invented by the Swiss as a way of using up some of their spare milk. Large-scale production of dairy milk chocolate was pioneered in Britain. The process of making it involves mixing chocolate and sugar with concentrated milk.

16. The great diet debate

Not all that many years ago, people who had been ill were advised to drink lots of milk and eat plenty of dishes with cream in them. For children, especially those from poor homes where the parents could not afford to buy all the proper food, milk was considered to be of special importance. It provided the substances they needed to grow, and milk was frequently issued free at schools all over the world.

Apart from the fact that it tasted good, butter was also regarded as being an essential part of a healthy diet, and dairy products in general were advertised as being especially healthy.

Nowadays, though, there are quite serious

So as not to end up like this man, many doctors now advise us to cut down on our butter consumption. Health-conscious people are eating more low-fat spreads.

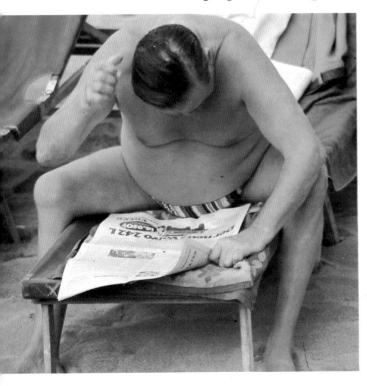 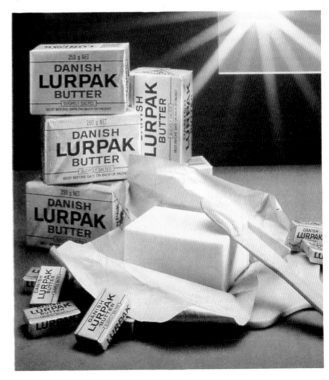

A tempting array of foods, but most of them contain cholesterol which many doctors now think causes heart disease.

doubts about the value of rich milk and butter. Many doctors say that both contain a substance known as cholesterol which can, if too much of it is absorbed into the body from a rich diet, clog up the arteries which carry our blood. Of course, doctors do not only blame dairy products: eggs, fat meats and certain cooking oils also contain cholesterol and these, too, are considered as possibly harmful.

The world's dairy industries reply that the good things in dairy products far outweigh any possible dangers to health. Even so, doctors continue to advise a diet in which certain fats are omitted. They also suggest that skimmed milk should be used instead of full cream, especially by people trying to lose weight.

The truth is probably that people in the industrialized countries simply eat too much of everything, while at the same time taking far too little exercise. Flabby, overweight people are naturally unhealthy, and they need to watch everything they eat more carefully than those who are slim and strong.

17. Lakes and mountains

Cheddar cheese being made in New Zealand, in one of the largest factories in the world. Britain used to import about 75 per cent of New Zealand's cheese exports. Since joining the EEC, she only imports about 10 per cent.

Like many other commodities, there is a large trade world-wide in dairy products, much of it being transported in refrigerated ships. New Zealand, for example, eats more butter per head than any other nation but little of the cheese that she produces, so most of it is exported. Britain used to import 75 per cent of it until she became a member of the European Economic Community (EEC). Now she imports only 10 per cent of New Zealand's cheese.

This is a result of the EEC's Common Agricultural Policy, which aims to give European farmers a fair income and to keep prices in shops stable. One of the ways it does this is by taxing any agricultural produce that is imported into the EEC from non-member countries, such as New Zealand.

Under the Common Agricultural Policy, all agricultural produce in the EEC is given a fixed

Butter from an EEC 'mountain' is usually sold off at a cheaper price than normal.

Containers of Danish butter being unloaded at a British port.

price. If too much butter, for instance, is made, its price will fall below the fixed price. If this happens, the EEC buys the butter and stores it until the price begins to rise again. This system can encourage farmers to produce too much of a product and has led to the creation of what have been described as butter 'mountains' and wine and milk 'lakes'.

In an effort to stop the creation of these surpluses, the EEC often imposes strict quotas on the amount of a particular product that can be produced. Dairy farmers, for example, have had strict quotas imposed on milk production. As a result, many farmers have had to kill some of their milking cows and a few have even had to give up farming because they cannot afford to switch to another form of agriculture.

39

18. Dairy organizations

The dairy industry world-wide is organized on a local and international basis. Many nations, like Canada, have orgainizations which control the distribution of milk, give advice on running dairy farms, check cattle for disease, and make sure that farmers are getting a fair price for their dairy products.

In Britain, for example, there is the Milk Marketing Board. Set up in 1933, it is financed totally by money from farmers and arranges the sale of milk from the farm to the dairy. No farm milk can be sold by anyone else. The Milk Marketing Board provides a wide range of services, not the least of which is to encourage people to drink more milk, for milk producers face very fierce competition from other soft drinks, like colas, fruit juices, tea and coffee. So the Milk Marketing Board organizes large promotion campaigns in magazines and newspapers, and on roadside hoardings and on television,

This Milk Marketing Board tanker picks up milk from a farm and transports it to a dairy, where it is bottled or cartoned.

Fresh milk's gotta lotta bottle

Part of the job of the Milk Marketing Board in Britain is to encourage more people to drink milk.

encouraging everyone to drink more milk.

The Milk Marketing Board is one of the many national organizations that belong to the International Dairy Federation. Based in Brussels, in Belgium, this holds a congress every four years to discuss issues affecting the dairy industry around the world.

There are also several international bodies which help poorer nations with their agricultural problems. The Food and Agriculture Organization (FAO), part of the United Nations, gives aid and advice on increasing the production and use of milk in these areas. FAO employees teach farmers modern ways of milking and of looking after cows, and also advise on setting up dairies.

41

19. Strawberries or cream?

Many of the world's poorer countries are developing efficient dairy industries. This is a cheese factory in Kenya.

Many people agree that cattle ranching (raising enormous herds of cattle to be turned into beef) is a wasteful form of farming because the feedstuffs they eat might be better used if they were fed straight to hungry people. The whole subject can start fierce arguments between meat-eaters and vegetarians, but at least nobody ever claims that dairy farming is a waste of resources since dairy products are so obviously nutritious and economically produced.

As a result many of the world's poorer countries are encouraging their own farmers to try raising dairy cattle, but the results are not always happy. To begin with, dairy cows need a lot of often expensive care and attention, clean sheds and very complicated milking, pasteurizing, storage and bottling equipment, as well as refrigeration facilities. All these things have to be connected to cheap electricity supplies, and in many parts of the world even ordinary electric light is an unheard of luxury.

If they are to benefit the greatest number of people, dairy products also need to be transported quickly from the farms and creameries by rail or road tanker; many poor countries lack good road and rail networks. In the main, then, their dairy farms can only serve small regions.

There are exceptions, and India in particular is developing an efficient dairy industry, but in the meantime many developing countries limit themselves to growing fruit and vegetables which can be sold to wealthier nations for cash which can, in turn, be used by them to import dairy products.

In years to come things may change, but until

Inadequate road and rail communications are hampering the development of dairy industries in poorer nations.

they do, it is still often a case of the rich countries of the world saying to the poorer countries: 'You grow the strawberries, and we will provide the cream.'

43

Facts and figures

Top right *Foods which provide one-sixth (16.7 per cent) of a person's recommended daily amounts of any nutrients are considered to be a reasonable source of that nutrient. This table shows the proportion of recommended daily amounts supplied by a pint of milk.*

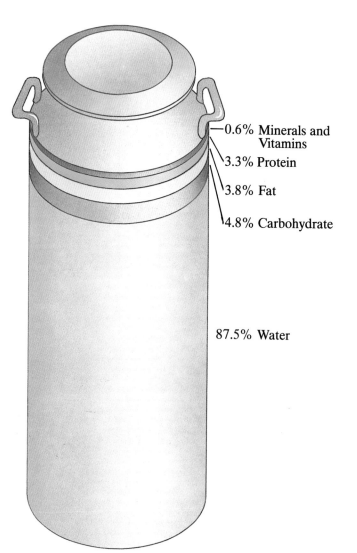

—0.6% Minerals and Vitamins

3.3% Protein

3.8% Fat

4.8% Carbohydrate

87.5% Water

Left *This diagram gives a breakdown of the ingredients that make up milk.*

Bottom right *This table shows the top fifteen milk-producing countries in the world. The figures show how much milk they produce each year.*

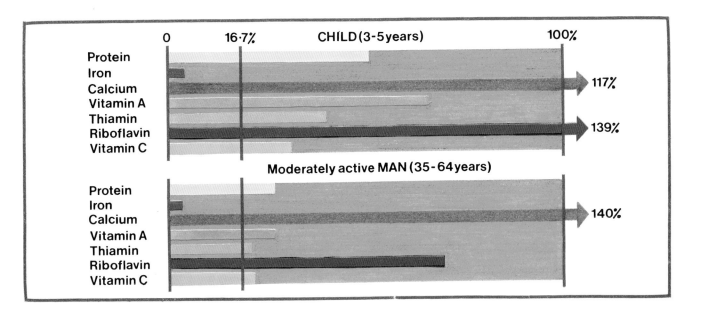

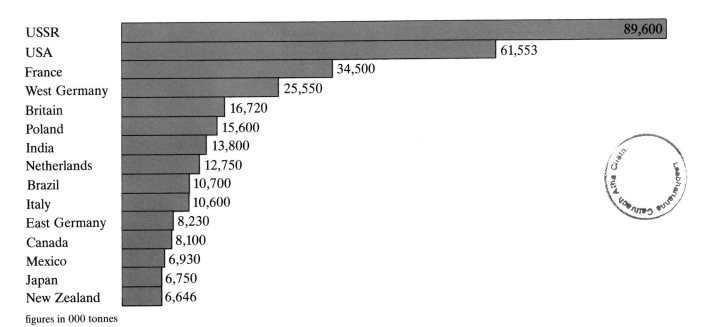

USSR	89,600
USA	61,553
France	34,500
West Germany	25,550
Britain	16,720
Poland	15,600
India	13,800
Netherlands	12,750
Brazil	10,700
Italy	10,600
East Germany	8,230
Canada	8,100
Mexico	6,930
Japan	6,750
New Zealand	6,646

figures in 000 tonnes

Glossary

Abomasum The fourth stomach of a cow, where food is finally broken down by the digestive juices.

Aerosol A can containing gas under pressure which, when the button on top of the can is pressed, forces a substance, like cream, out.

Bacteria Tiny organisms which exist in millions of different varieties, and can do good as well as cause harm.

Billion In many countries, a billion used to be one million million units. Now most countries use the USA's measure of one thousand million units.

Bovine An adjective meaning of or like cattle.

Brucellosis An infectious disease in cows.

Butterchurn The simplest type is in the form of a barrel with a lid. It has a handle which operates two perforated paddles inside the barrel and the churning motion produces the butter.

Cholesterol A sticky substance which exists in large quantities in animal fats and dairy products. It can coat the walls of veins and cause heart and other health problems.

Concentrates Food in a highly compact form.

Cud A ball of half-chewed food brought up from a cow's rumen (see below) to be munched up.

Curd When rennet (see below) or acids are added to milk, it solidifies into soft lumps, called curds. The thin liquid which is drained from them is called whey.

Domesticate To tame wild animals.

Emulsifiers Chemicals which help to thicken liquids or some foods, like ice-cream, and keep them thick at ordinary room temperature.

Glands Small organs in human and animal bodies which stimulate various bodily functions, and can also act on the brain.

Gourd Containers which are used for carrying liquids, usually made from marrow-like vegetables which have been dried in the sun.

Homogenization A process in which the fat globules in milk are broken down in size by forcing them through a series of tiny holes.

Nomads People who have no settled home, but travel from one area to another, usually in search of fresh fodder for their animals.

Nutritional Food products which supply all or some of the minerals, vitamins and carbohydrates needed in a healthy diet.

Omasum The third stomach of a cow, where surplus water is removed from the food.

Pasteurization A process in which harmful bacteria in milk are killed by heating it to 70°C (158°F) for several seconds.

Peasant A very poor farmer who uses out-of-date farming methods and so can only produce a small amount of goods for sale.

Ranching Rearing cattle on a large scale on vast farms, like on the prairies in Canada and the USA, and the pampas in Argentina.

Rennet An acid, taken from the stomach of a calf, which curdles milk to make cheese.

Reticulum The second stomach of a cow, where half-eaten food can be stored before being brought up for chewing.

Rinderpest An infectious disease which causes fever and dysentery in cud-chewing animals.

Rumen The first stomach of a cow, where half-eaten food is stored on the way to the reticulum.

Sterilization Killing of germs by boiling or by treating with chemicals.

Tuberculosis A disease of cattle and humans in which small growths appear in the lungs.

Books to read

DEVENISH, R. *Mr Bourne is a Milkman* (Young Library, 1983)
DOGANIS, S. *The Milk Run* (Hamilton, 1976)
HINDS, L. *Butter and Margarine* (Watts, 1982)
INGVES, G. *Cows* (Black, 1982)
PATTERSON, G. *Dairy Farming* (Deutsch, 1983)
PITT, V. *Cheese* (Watts, 1982)
STADTLER, C. *A Day with a Milkman* (Wayland, 1984)
STEWART, A. *The Milkman* (Hamilton, 1983)
WHITLOCK, R. *Dairy Cows* (Wayland, 1982)
The Milk Year (National Dairy Council)

Picture acknowledgements

The author and the publishers would like to thank the following for allowing their illustrations to be reproduced in this book: Butter Information Council 6, 22 (both), 23 (both), 39 (top); Camerapix Hutchison Library 7 (right/Sarah Errington), 8 (Brian Moser), 9, 10, 36 (left), 43 (Margaret Murray); Bruce Coleman Ltd 30; Danish Dairy Board *frontispiece*, 36 (right); Chris Fairclough *cover*, 20 (top), 25 (bottom), 26, 31, 33, 35; Preben Kristensen 28 (both), 29 (both); Milk Marketing Board of England and Wales 7 (left), 25 (top), 27, 40, 41; TOPHAM 20 (bottom), 39 (bottom), 42; United Dairies 16, 21; Wayland Picture Library 11 (both), 12, 13, 17 (both), 19 (top), 24, 34 (both), 37, 38. The diagrams on pages 14 (both), 15 (both), 18, 19 (bottom), 45 (top) are by Cecilia Packham-Head and the ones on pages 44 and 45 (bottom) are by Malcolm S. Walker.

Index

Africa 8
Asia 27
Australia 30

Bacteria 13, 28, 32
Britain 16, 20, 30, 35
Bulgaria 32
Butter 7, 26, 36, 37
    clarified 23
    consumption of 39
    discovery of 11
    making 13, 14, 15, 22–3
    'mountains' 39
Butterfat 6, 18
Buttermilk 23, 25

Canada 30, 40
Cheese 7, 8, 10
    consumption of 39
    making 11, 13, 14, 15, 28–9
    types 29, 30
Chocolate 35
Cholesterol 37
Common Agricultural Policy
    39
Condensed milk 21
Cows 7, 8
    breeds of 18
    stomach of 18
Cream 7, 11, 20, 22, 23, 36, 37
    artificial 27
    double 24
    single 24
    sour 25
    whipping 25
Curds 10, 28, 29

Dairies 15, 16
    hygiene in 13, 16

Dairy farming 14–15, 39, 43
Denmark 14, 30
Diet 7, 8, 32, 36–7
Diseases 8
    brucellosis 13
    rinderpest 20
    tuberculosis 13
Distributing milk 13, 16

Egypt 11
Evaporated milk 21
Europe 20, 27
EEC 39

Food and Agriculture
    Organization (FAO) 41
France 8, 13, 30

Ghee 23
Goats 8

Health 7, 32, 36–7
Homogenization 20, 21, 35
Horses 8

Ice-cream 34, 35
India 8
International Dairy Federation
    41
Ireland 14
Italy 8, 30, 34

Mammals 6
Margarine 26–7
Milk bottles 10, 16
Milk cartons 16, 20
Milking 10
    by hand 14, 18
    by machine 14, 18

Milk 'lakes' 39
Milk Marketing Board 40–41
Milk sugar 6
Milk tankers 16
Minerals 6
Mongolia 8

Netherlands 14, 30
New Zealand 14, 16, 30, 39

Pasteur, Louis 13
'Pasteurization' 13, 16, 20, 35
Powdered milk 20
Protein 6

Rennet 10, 28

Salt 11
Saudi Arabia 8
Sheep 8
Skimmed milk 37
Smetana 25
South America 8, 14
Sterilized milk 20
Sugar 6, 21
Switzerland 8, 30, 35

Ultra Heat Treatment (UHT)
    milk 20
USSR 8, 25, 32, 34
USA 8, 14, 20, 27, 30

Vitamins 6

Water buffalo 8
Whey 28, 32

Yaks 8
Yoghurt 32